ANAESTHETIC AND SEDATIVE TECHNIQUES FOR FISH

by

LINDSAY G. ROSS B.Sc. Ph.D.
BARBARA ROSS B.Sc. Ph.D.

INSTITUTE OF AQUACULTURE
UNIVERSITY OF STIRLING
STIRLING, FK9 4LA
SCOTLAND

1984

First Edition 1984

ISBN 0 901636 52 5

© 1984—Published by Institute of Aquaculture, University of Stirling, Scotland

Printed and bound by Brown, Son & Ferguson, Ltd., The Nautical Press, Glasgow G41 2SD

CONTENTS

PREFACE

The purpose of this handbook is to draw together the available information on sedation and anaesthesia of fishes. Both temperate and tropical freshwater species are considered as well as sedation in sea water. While sedation is a routine and essentially simple procedure it can also be mismanaged. The overall intention is therefore to produce an illustrated, practical guide for workers both in aquaculture and in research.

ACKNOWLEDGEMENTS

This handbook is one of a series produced by the Institute of Aquaculture of the University of Stirling to provide practical, readily available sources of information on various aspects of temperate and tropical aquaculture.

Some information presented here was generated while the authors were involved with the tropical aquaculture programme supported at Stirling by the Overseas Development Administration. Much of the remaining data is based on our own experience and that of many of our colleagues at Stirling over the last 10 years and we are grateful to all concerned for useful discussions and collaboration.

Thanks are also due to Lyn North for the cover graphics.

LIST OF TABLES

LIST OF FIGURES

CHAPTER 1

Introduction

The handling of fish both in and out of their natural environment almost always creates great difficulties. Their characteristic struggling during capture and handling usually has strong effects on both physiology and behaviour, and consequently it is often necessary to immobilise fish before attempting to perform even the most simple task (Tytler and Hawkins, 1981).

In the operation of a culture facility it is rarely necessary to sedate or anaesthetise stocks. For certain procedures however, and in research or veterinary work, sedation may be essential to minimise stress and physical damage and in some cases full surgical anaesthesia may be required. It should be noted that sedative and anaesthetic procedures may themselves induce undesirable side-effects although their advantages generally outweigh their disadvantages if the correct technique is used and sufficient control is maintained.

Almost any stimulus presented to a fish causes one or more of a number of behavioural and physiological changes collectively referred to as stress. Such stress may be counter-productive in the laboratory and in aquaculture it can lead to immediate or delayed mortalities and often causes poor feeding reactions for a day or so with consequent slower growth.

When fish are removed from water, individually or in groups, physiological stress is compounded by the risk of serious abrasion and mechanical shock, particularly with a struggling animal. Procedures which can be carried out entirely in water such as simple tagging, grading using screens or pumped water systems and batch weighing in water are unlikely to cause serious trauma and sedation is then unnecessary. Furthermore, careful handling of brood-stock can enable procedures such as stripping of eggs and sperm without sedation. Allison (1961) has shown that sperm motility was greatly reduced in brook trout at 19 mg.l^{-1} MS222, and clearly it is inadvisable to expose gametes to anaesthetics. For length-weight studies, sexing, simple injection, withdrawal of body fluids, branding and certain types of tagging sedation may be necessary, whereas for gonadectomy, hypophysectomy and tissue biopsy full surgical anaesthesia may be required.

1

Another less obvious area where sedation is beneficial is in bulk transportation of stocks, particularly over long distances. Apart from minimising direct physical injury and stress effects during transportation, sedation is useful in reducing metabolic rate and consequently oxygen consumption, and in reducing excretion of metabolic products into the water.

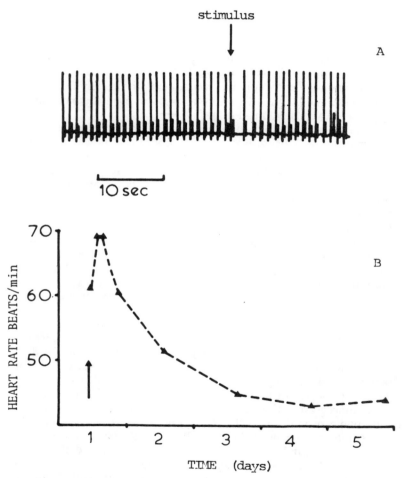

Fig. 1. The effects of stress on heart rate in saithe (*Pollachius virens*).
 (a) Momentary bradycardia caused by observer appearing at side of tank.
 (b) Chronic tachycardia following anaesthesia and implantation of ECG electrodes.

Over the last 20 yr a considerable amount of work has been carried out on stress in fishes (e.g., Wedemeyer, 1970; Wardle, 1972; Wardle and Kanwisher, 1974; Casillas and Smith, 1977; Soivio *et al.*, 1977; Ross and Ross, 1983; Yaron, *et al.*, 1983) and although much literature exists on the subject, only limited generalisations can be made. Stress responses are induced in fishes by changes in their environment and by netting and handling, and because of this it is almost impossible to investigate the physiology of an unstressed fish other than by remote sensing techniques such as telemetry.

There are a number of characteristic external signs of stress in fish including ataxia, obvious tachyventilation and marked colour change which can either be darkening or blanching.

At the simplest physiological level stress may inhibit a single heartbeat in response to a momentary stimulus (fig. 1a). More severe stress may, however, produce very prolonged effects which may or may not revert to normal for more than 24 hr. Short duration bradycardia may be replaced by tachycardia, often of long duration, for example, Figure 1b shows the effects on heart rate of simple ECG electrode implantation in saithe (*Pollachius virens*). Clearly cardiac rate and ventilatory rate are functionally linked and in many circumstances they can be synchronised neuronally (Randall, 1970). It has been shown by Serfaty *et al.*, (1959) and Houston *et al.*, (1971) that MS222 (Tricaine methanesulphonate) induction produces both tachycardia and tachyventilation. Ventilatory and respiratory parameters are good indicators of stress, and although the causes are not fully understood cough rate has been found to be a better indicator than other general respiratory changes (Sprague, 1971). Figure 2 demonstrates the effects of formalin treatment on ventilation rate and cough rate of rainbow trout (*Salmo gairdneri*).

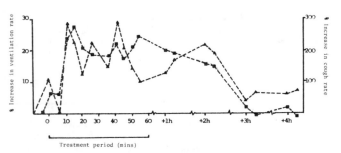

FIG. 2. The effects of a standard prophylactic 200 ppm formalin treatment on ventilation rate and cough rate of rainbow trout (*Salmo gairdneri*).
Triangles, ventilation rate; squares, cough rate.

There are a number of well-documented haematological effects induced by stress. These may include haemoconcentration or haemodilution, swelling of erythrocytes and increase or decrease of osmolarity, plasma chloride, sodium, potassium and other ion levels. Smith (1982) has summarised the work of numerous authors to show the direction of change for a variety of physiological functions under the influence of different stressors. These factors clearly also affect osmoregulatory capability.

Most of the components of any general stress response can be divided into 2 groups. The catecholamines epinephrine and norepinephrine, released by the sympathetic nervous system, produce a series of significant changes which are summarised in Table 1. These changes may begin in less than a second and can last for many minutes up to a few hours.

Release of cortisol from the interrenal bodies in the head kidney begins in under an hour but may continue for weeks or even months

TABLE 1   The effects of catecholamine and corticosteroid release during stress in fishes. Data drawn from the work of numerous authors

Catecholamines	1.	Increased blood glucose.
(*Epinephrine and*	2.	Increased blood lactate
Norepinephrine)	3.	Changes in free fatty acids.
	4.	Tachycardia and increased cardiac output.
	5.	Tachyventilation.
	6.	Vasodilation or vasoconstriction.
	7.	Increase in haematocrit.
	8.	Glucogenesis in liver and muscle.
	9.	Increased peristalsis.

Cortisol	1.	Protein mobilisation.
(*or Cortisone*)	2.	Increased protein synthesis.
	3.	Inhibition of growth.
	4.	Reduced utilisation of carbohydrate.
	5.	Increased glucose production from tissue protein.
	6.	Deposition of glycogen in the liver.
	7.	Changes in membrane permeability.
	8.	Increased production of and activity of Na/K-ATPase.

(Smith, 1982). Its effects are wide-ranging, often deleterious and are also summarised in Table 1. Its main effect appears to be an increase in permeability of membranes to ions and its production due to stress has been well described by Wedemeyer (1969), Fagerlund and Donaldson (1970), Fryer (1975), Singly and Chavin (1975) and Yaron *et al.*, (1983). Figure 3 shows the typical rise in serum cortisol induced by stress.

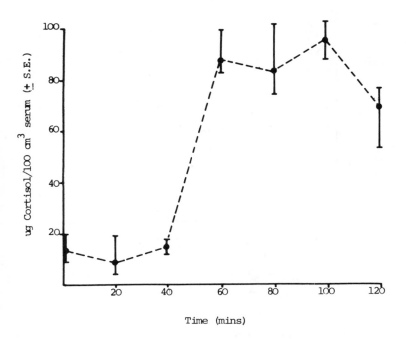

FIG. 3. Cortisol production in *Oncorhynchus kisutch* stressed by stirring the aquarium water. (After Wedemeyer, 1969.)

Anaesthesia itself induces stress reactions although it is difficult to distinguish the direct effects of the drug from those of capture or handling. Randall and Smith (1976) demonstrated the magnitude of the cardio-ventilatory effects of MS222 anaesthesia in rainbow trout (fig. 4) and Houston et al., (1971) in a comparable study showed that dorsal aortic blood pressure was similarly affected. Despite this it is clear that anaesthetics are necessary in many cases to limit the magnitude of the stress response in addition to facilitating handling.

A range of techniques are avaliable for the sedation or anaesthesia of fishes in differing circumstances, and this book attempts to describe the various approaches and the current state of the art.

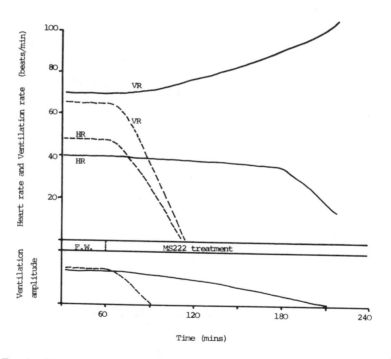

Fig. 4.   Changes in heart rate, ventilation rate and ventilation amplitude at 2 levels of MS222 anaesthesia. Dotted lines 150 mg.l^{-1}; solid lines 75 mg.l^{-1}. (After Randall and Smith, 1967.)

CHAPTER 2

Factors affecting response of fish to anaesthesia

Anaesthetic procedures usually act by widespread depression of the central nervous system produced by an action on nerve axons, transmitter release or membrane exitability. It should be noted that little is known about the precise mode of action in fish although with some drugs there appears to be an inverse relationship between the dose level required to induce a given depth of anaesthesia and the animals evolutionary status. Consequently a fish would require a larger dose of a drug than a mammal to produce a given effect. It has been suggested that this phenomenon is due to an increasing presence of active sites in higher vertebrates.

When induction is slow a series of stages of anaesthesia can be observed and these have been described for fishes by McFarland (1959). His scheme is reproduced in Table 2 and it can be seen that an anaesthetic substance can produce sedation, surgical anaesthesia or narcotic death, depending on the dose level and the length of exposure. In practise it is often found that a species may not conform to every aspect of McFarland's description.

Desirable features of an anaesthetic agent
Broadly there are 3 main approaches to the sedation and anaesthesia

TABLE 2   Stages of anaesthesia in fish. After McFarland (1959)

Stage	Plane	Description	Behavioural signs
I	1	Light sedation	Responsive to stimuli but motion reduced, ventilation decreased.
I	2	Deep sedation	As above, some analgesia, only receptive to gross stimulation.
II	1	Light anaesthesia	Partial loss of equilibrium. Good analgesia.
II	2	Deeper anaesthesia	Total loss of muscle tone, total loss of equilibrium, ventilation almost absent.
III		Surgical anaesthesia	As above; total loss of reaction to even massive stimulation.
IV		Medullary collapse	Ventilation ceases, cardiac arrest, eventual death. Overdose.

7

of fish, namely the use of drugs and gases, induction of hypothermia or exposure to an electric current.

It is preferable that a sedative or anaesthetic drug or gas should be effective at low doses and that the toxic dose should considerably exceed the effective dose providing a wide safety margin. It is also desirable that the chemicals do not produce hyperactivity during induction. In addition, the substance should be easily soluble in water or a water-soluble solvent, should be easy to obtain in bulk and should be safe to operators. Since in aquaculture and fisheries large numbers of animals are frequently handled it is often necessary to dispense large quantities of drugs which may not remain effective in working solution for more than 24 hr or so. Consequently, where the drug is unstable or degraded over a short period cost becomes important.

When fish are immobilised by lowering of temperature, the main consideration is that the rate of cooling and the required reduced temperature can both be controlled.

Fish can be immobilised using various forms of electric current and in addition to the general considerations described for chemicals, operator safety is of paramount importance.

Finally, no matter which technique is used, the required level of sedation or anaesthesia should be easily reversed without prolonged ataxia or other undesirable features.

Factors affecting response of fish to anaesthesia
In common with anaesthesia of other animals there is a series of factors which can alter or mediate the efficacy of anaesthetic processes in fish. These can broadly be divided into biological and environmental factors and they are summarised in Table 3.

Unlike other distinct vertebrate taxa the fishes are very diverse

TABLE 3   Factors affecting the efficacy of anaesthetics for fish

Biological factors	Species: gill area body weight ratio.
	Size and weight: metabolic rate.
	Lipid content: oily fish or older specimens.
	Sex and sexual maturity: lipid content.
	Body condition: exhausted, post-spawners.
	Disease status.
Environmental factors	Temperature: poikilotherm.
	pH: ionisation of molecules.
	Salinity: buffering.
	Mineral content of environment: calcium antagonism.

both in body shape and detailed design. A 100 g trout for example has a very different body shape and a greater gill area than an eel of similar weight. Consequently, they are unlikely to respond similarly to a given anaesthetic treatment. Often the rate at which anaesthetic drugs become effective can be related to gill area to body weight ratios and these can vary considerably between species. Indeed in some species, for example certain air breathers, the gills are reduced to a single arch used only for osmoregulation and excretion. From a knowledge of body structure it is usually possible to predict how a given species may respond.

Within a species, there is a direct relationship between drug dose and size (Houston and Woods, 1972; Huish, 1972). This general observation suggests that metabolic rates are in some way equal, whereas in fact there is an inverse relationship between metabolic rate and body weight. In practise, large active fish within a group often succumb to chemical anaesthesia before their smaller counterparts and in tilapia it has been noted that fry anaesthetised along with much larger fish recover surprisingly rapidly from the effects of the drug (Ross and Geddes, 1979).

Many drugs such as MS222 and benzocaine are fat soluble. Thus, in larger, older fish or in gravid females duration of anaesthesia may be prolonged and consequent recovery slower.

In common with all vertebrates diseased or exhausted animals are very susceptible to anaesthetic treatment. Schoettger and Steuke (1970) showed that pike (*Esox lucius*) and walleye (*Stizostedion vitreum*) depleted after spawning were more susceptible to MS222. Richards (pers. comm.) found that sea trout with saprolegnia did not recover reliably from anaesthesia.

Fish culturists are often concerned about the repeated use of anaesthetics and their possible effects on fish growth and performance. McFarland and Klontz (1969) claim that the careful and proper use of tertiary amyl alcohol, methyl pentynol and MS222 is unattended by side effects even with repeated use. Nakatani (1962) induced deep MS222 anaesthesia ($100 \, mg.l^{-1}$) in trout 5 times per week for 21 weeks and noted no side effects. In addition, Ross and Geddes (1979) described regular use of benzocaine on tilapia with no apparent reduction in growth or spawning ability.

The body temperatures of fish closely follow that of their environment because of highly efficient heat exchange in the gills. Consequently, the effects of temperature on anaesthetic dose can be considerable. Unfortunately, there is no simple underlying relationship and the effect is entirely dependent on the type of drug used. With MS222 and benzocaine higher doses are required at higher temperatures to produce the same effect. It has been suggested that this is due to these non-hydrogen binding anaesthetics stabilising the micro crystals of the encephalonic fluids (Pauling, 1961; Cherkin and Catchpool, 1964). Sehdev et al., (1963) showed a similar effect for 2-phenoxyethanol and they also showed that its therapeutic index was increased at lower temperatures. Obviously physico-chemical passage of the drug into the fish is also temperature related.

The pH of an anaesthetic solution will influence its efficacy, possibly by affecting the ratio of charged to uncharged molecules. In addition a medium of low pH (e.g., unbuffered MS222; pH 3·8 at $30\,mg.l^{-1}$) induces a stress reaction. Quinaldine, a base with a pKa of 5·42, forms increasingly ionised solutions as the pH falls and loses its anaesthetic efficacy.

Because of the buffering capacity of seawater and its ionic constituents the effects of some drugs may be modified, even in the same species. In general most anaesthetic drugs are effective in seawater but the barbiturates are antagonised by high calcium levels (McFarland and Klontz, 1969).

Although it is useful for operators to be aware of these mitigating factors, it is not always possible to take account of them in a predictable way. The cumulative effects of these variations are most easily seen when anaesthetising batches of fish when it becomes obvious that some individuals respond very differently from the bulk of their fellows.

CHAPTER 3

Inhalation anaesthesia

This most widely used technique depends on the anaesthetic drug being in aqueous solution. It is ventilated (inhaled) by the fish and enters the arterial blood from where it is a very short route to the central nervous system (fig. 5). This is analogous to gaseous anaesthesia in terrestrial vertebrates. On return to fresh water the drugs, or their metabolites, are excreted via the gills.

There are certain species of fish which can breathe air rendering this technique unsatisfactory. The snakehead (*Ophiocephalus spp.*) is an example of an obligate air breather and its gills are much reduced, being used only for excretion and osmoregulatory purposes. Consequently, although the animal does respond to inhalation anaesthesia, induction is usually lengthy, unpredictable and therefore frustrating. The eel (*Anguilla anguilla*) and most catfishes are facultative air breathers and when placed in noxious solutions have a tendency to hold their breath. In this case although induction is lengthy it is nevertheless effective.

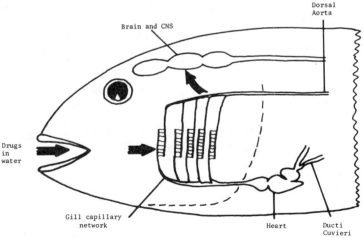

FIG. 5.   Route of inhaled drugs to central nervous system of fish.

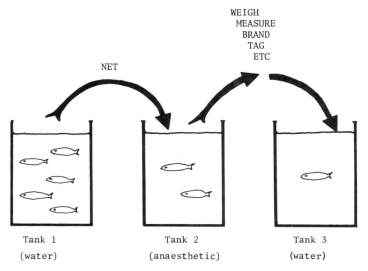

FIG. 6.   Schematic representation of simple inhalation anaesthesia procedure as used in fisheries and aquaculture.

For simple procedures it is usually possible to immerse the fish directly in a suitable concentration of drugs so that spontaneous ventilation is maintained, and this approach is widely use in fish farming. The simplest method of achieving this is to make up the required drug concentration in a container and to quickly but gently transfer the fish to the container. For most procedures in aquaculture and fisheries management this technique is quite adequate and fish can be transferred to clean water within a few minutes having been weighed, measured, marked or whatever (fig. 6; app. 1). Using this procedure it is usually not necessary to exceed stage 1 plane 2 of McFarland's scheme (table 2) for adequate handling.

Unfortunately it is difficult to maintain an uniform depth of anaesthesia using this technique. For example Houston *et al.*, (1971) have shown that levels of MS222 in brain and muscle continue to increase after blood levels have attained equilibrium. Consequently, a drug dose which is initially satisfactory can produce progressively deeper anaesthesia and eventual ventilatory arrest. The resulting decline of water flow in the buccal cavity contributes to a reflex decline in heart rate and dorsal aortic blood pressure. A progressive hypoxia ensues which is further complicated in some cases by swelling of erythrocytes causing a decrease in gill capillary blood flows (Soivio *et al.*, 1977). Species with a high body lipid content, or large mature fish, retain fat-soluble anaesthetic agents for a longer period after recovery. During simple procedures these complications will not occur but it will readily be appreciated that lengthy exposure to a dissolved anaesthetic agent should be avoided. In more complex work, where ventilatory arrest is unavoidable, a system of artificial ventilation should be used.

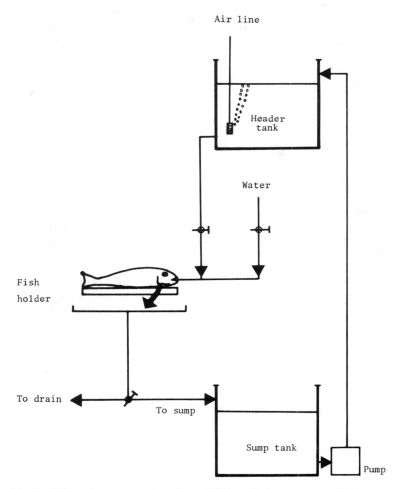

Fig. 7. Schematic representation of an artificial ventilation system suitable for more prolonged procedures.

Numerous descriptions of appropriate systems for ventilated anaesthesia exist in the literature (Bell, 1964). All that is required is a supply of anaesthetic solution at the correct temperature delivered from a pipe or mouthpiece into the buccal cavity and preferably a recycling system for used solution. The anaesthetic should be aerated to remove dissolved CO_2 and maintained at the correct temperature (fig. 7). The fish is first sedated in a container of appropriate anaesthetic solution and is then transferred to a suitable fish holder on an apparatus containing the maintenance solution. It is most convenient to cover the fish holder with some soft, wettable, disposable material which does not readily disintegrate. Similarly, wetted operation cloths may be desirable for shielding the fish from the heat of lights etc. It is also helpful to use a routine ECG monitor, for example an oscilloscope and pre-amplifier or else a simple bleeper triggered by the QRS complex (Ross and Wiewiorka, 1977).

Depending on drugs used and environmental control, fish can be held in this state for several hours. Clearly in this situation the 2 prime complicating factors are body temperature maintenance and prevention of excessive drying of the skin. The former is usually alleviated by adequate control of the water temperature, and the latter by spraying the skin surface with water at regular intervals from a wash bottle or small portable atomiser.

To terminate anaesthesia the supply is stopped and water is passed over the gills until spontaneous ventilation returns. At first appearance of locomotor activity the fish may be returned to the stock tank. Those wishing to anaesthetise fish of any value should always anticipate ventilatory arrest and its ensuing complications. It is helpful to remember the ventilatory/cardiac reflex in this context and by simply irrigating the buccal cavity continuously with water, heart rate can be maintained and excretion of drugs back across the gills can be speeded up.

Drugs used in inhalation anaesthesia
A wide range of drugs have been used as fish anaesthetics (Stuart, 1979). Some of these are no longer popular, for example urethane which has been found to be carcinogenic (Wood, 1956). In many cases their usefulness is limited by the lack of knowledge of their precise physiological effects. This description will be limited to those substances currently in wide usage but Table 4 gives an indication of the range of chemicals which have been used.

(a) *2-Phenoxyethanol*   This is an oily liquid which passes into solution if shaken with a small quantity of water. Doses of $0.5 \, cm^3.l^{-1}$ $(385 \, mg.l^{-1})$ produce surgical anaesthesia in rainbow trout and

TABLE 4   A compilation of drugs effective in inducing anaesthesia in fish by inhalation

Tricaine methane sulphonate (MS222) All four in wide use. Benzocaine Quinaldine (and quinaldine sulphate) 2-Phenoxyethanol	
Choral hydrate Tertiary amyl alcohol Methyl parafynol Chloroform Tribromoethanol Chlorbutanol	Effective but with side-effects, now not very widely used.
Sodium amytal Sodium pentobarbitone	Effective and in occassional use.
4-Styrylpyridine Diethyl ether Seccobarbital Piscaine Propoxate Urethane*	Have been used in isolated cases. *Urethane was very widely used and effective but now known to be carcinogenic.

sedation can be produced at a lower dose although analgesia is sometimes incomplete. Recovery is abrupt on occasions. The solution is bacteriocidal and fungicidal and because of this additional feature it is useful during laparotomy or abdominal surgery. It remains effective in working solution for at least 3 days.

(b) *Quinaldine*   This is an oily liquid which must be dissolved in acetone in order to mix with water. It is ineffective at pH 5 and below and is more potent at higher pH. While it is an effective anaesthetic it is irritant, insoluble and corneal damage has been reported following its use with salmonids (Richards, pers. comm.). Quinaldine sulphate is water soluble, but it is not easily available commercially (Blasiola, 1976). The low cost of quinaldine has made it a popular tool for collection of fishes from tidal pools and small lagoons.

(c) *MS222 (Tricaine methanesulphonate)*   This has been well investigated with many species. It is acidic and very soluble in water as a consequence. The low pH solution produced is irritant to fish, however, and a formidable list of physiological consequences to its use are documented. These include hypoxia, hypercapnia, hyperglycaemia, changes in blood electrolytes, hormones, cholesterol, urea, lactate and interrenal ascorbic acid. It should be borne in mind that handling alone can cause some of these changes. It is effective at 10–40 mg.l^{-1} in salmonids (Laird and Oswald, 1975) but up to 100 mg.l^{-1} is required for tilapias and *Clarias spp.* (Ross and Geddes, 1979).

(d) *Benzocaine* (*Ethyl-4-aminobenzoate*)   This is very similar to MS222, but is insoluble in water and must first be dissolved in acetone or ethanol. A stock solution can be prepared (usually 100 g.l^{-1}) which, if kept in a dark bottle, will keep for long periods (at least a year). It is easier and less wasteful to dispense small volumes of this stock than to weigh out small quantities of solids.

In solution, benzocaine is neutral, and causes a less stressful reaction than MS222 although many of the side effects are still present. The long term consequences of these side effects do not seem to impair function and regular anaesthesia at Stirling has not shown any decrement of growth or reproductive capacity.

Benzocaine is effective in approximately the same doses as MS222, it is relatively harmless to man and is effective with freshwater, marine and tropical species, again at higher doses in the latter.

(e) *Propoxate*   This drug has very impressive anaesthetic properties, being about 100 times more potent than MS222. Very rapid induction occurs at high doses (30–60s at 4 mg.l^{-1}), lower doses are effective but induction takes longer (5–9 min at 1 mg.l^{-1}). In addition, it is said to form a stable solution for long periods and has a high therapeutic index. Unfortunately the drug is extremely expensive and probably because of this little is known of its metabolism or effects.

CHAPTER 4

Parenteral anaesthesia

In some circumstances, particularly for surgery or lengthy procedures, parenteral anaesthesia may be preferable. The technique requires less specialised artificial ventilation apparatus than that required for inhalation anaesthesia. Usually the fish are rapidly sedated by inhalation anaesthesia to minimise handling stress, the animal is then weighed, the dose calculated and then injected.

Depending on the size of the fish, injection may be intraperitoneal, intravascular or intramuscular (fig. 8). Intraperitoneal injection is the most common and the use of a short, narrow gauge needle ventral to the lateral line will ensure access to the peritoneal cavity. This simple method involves absorption of the drug through visceral blood vessels and induction is consequently slow. In larger fish intravascular injection may be possible and using appropriate needles access may be gained to certain fin sinuses, the caudal artery and vein or by cannulation of the dorsal or ventral aortas. Small drug volumes can be very rapidly absorbed if introduced into the red lateral muscle but this technique is only possible in those species having a sub-

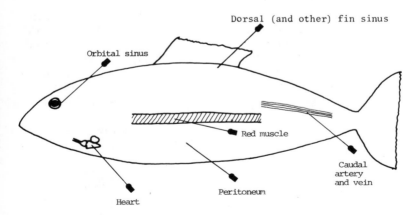

FIG. 8.   Injection sites available for parenteral administration of drugs. Note that not all sites will be available in a given species.

TABLE 5   A compilation of drugs effective in inducing anaesthesia in fish when administered parenterally

Alphaxolone	(Saffan)	Very good; long duration.
Propanidid	(Epontol)	
Ketamine-HCl	(Vetalar)	
Xylazine-HCl	(Rompun)	
Etorphine/acetylpromazine	(Immobilon)	Used sequentially.
Diprenorphine-HCl	(Revivon)	
Sodium pentabarbitone	(Nembutal)	Long duration.
Sodium amylobarbitone	(Amytal)	
Sodium methohexitone	(Brevital)	Short duration.
Sodium thiopentone	(Pentothal)	
Lignocaine-HCl		Spinal anaesthesia only.
Procaine-HCl		Local analgesic only.

stantial block of red muscle. The 10 times greater blood flow in red muscle ensures rapid induction although precautions must be taken to eliminate reflux of the drug from the injection site.

A number of drugs have been used parenterally, and these are summarised in Table 5. It is interesting to note that both benzocaine and MS222 are ineffective when given parenterally, probable because the rate of uptake is effectively lower than the gill clearance rate. Very little work has been carried out on injectable fish anaesthetics and effective practical anaesthesia is probably limited to the following 3 drugs.

(a) Nembutal (*Sodium pentobarbitone*)

This is easily available as an injectable solution, it is very stable and effective at doses of 48–72 mg.kg^{-1} intraperitoneal. Anaesthesia is very lengthy, extending from 6–24 hr depending on dose (Oswald, 1978). the main complications are that recovery is very prolonged, there is usually intense bradycardia, ventilatory arrest and the drug has some curare-like properties. By contrast, in some elasmobranchs nembutal is effective at 6 mg.kg^{-1} but fatal at 60 mg.kg^{-1} (Walker, 1972). Unlike most other anaesthetic agents this drug is not excreted by the gills to any great extent which may explain its long action. Initial recovery is probably by redistribution within the fish.

(b) Propanidid (*Eponotol*)

Although doses of 8–9 mg.kg^{-1} are effective in producing very short anaesthesia in mammals (Clarke and Dundee, 1966) intraperitoneal doses of 325 mg.kg^{-1} are required for effective anaesthesia in rainbow trout and its action lasts for about 2·5 hr (Oswald, 1978). Its chief advantages are that it does not greatly depress ventilation and recovery is comparatively uneventful.

(b) Alphaxolone (*Saffan*)

This is an excellent drug for long-term anaesthesia and in recent years has been adopted by fish neurophysiologists because spontaneous nervous activity is essentially preserved. Its main advantage lies in its stimulatory effect upon the heart, heart beat becoming very regular and forceful. In addition, it has a general vasodilatory effect both systemically and peripherally, and this ensures adequate oxygenation of the blood. At low doses $(12\,mg.kg^{-1})$ it is possible to maintain respiration and circulation at approximately the basal level in cod (Tytler and Hawkins, 1981). With higher doses however, (over $24\,mg.kg^{-1}$ in rainbow trout) ventilation becomes reciprocatory and may be abolished altogether (Oswald, 1978). Consequently, it is always advisable to anticipate ventilatory arrest. Neuromuscular preparations give consistent results over long periods using this anaesthetic. It can also be extremely valuable in studies of the cardiovascular system (Ross, unpublished data).

It is important to bear in mind that many commercially available injectable preparations contain additives such as bacteriocides, detergents, solvents or stabilisers. It is thus necessary to exercise caution so that these components do not damage the gills where recovery is important. For example, both epontol and saffan contain the powerful surfactant "Cremophor EL".

CHAPTER 5

Other chemical methods

There are certain other chemical methods of anaesthesia which have limited use. These are the incorporation of chemicals into the feed and the use of dissolved narcotic gases.

Chemicals in food

This method is relatively stress-free and has been used by Takeshi Murai *et al.*, (1979) who fed pellets containing diazepam to American shad (*Alosa sapidissima*). Although at first sight this method is very attractive there are certain problems which include the technicalities of incorporating the material in the diet. Furthermore, induction will tend to be slow as the drug is absorbed via the gut and it is not possible to predict accurately the quantity consumed by individuals in the tank.

Use of gases

Gaseous anaesthesia as such is virtually impossible with fish since the fine gill lamellae collapse and fold out of water which increases the diffusion distance and decreases the exchange area (Alexander, 1967). Consequently, only gases which are relatively soluble in water can be considered for most fish. Only in fish which are capable of aerial respiration, such as catfish which have modified brush-like lamellae which do not collapse in air, one-gilled eels, the Symbranchidae, and fish with modified lungs such as *Amphipnous cuchia* could gaseous anaesthesia be considered feasible. It should be noted however, that even in these cases it has not been tried or tested.

The anaesthetic properties of CO_2 are well documented and it has been used with almost every animal phylum. In fish it is an effective anaesthetic but has only seen occasional use as a sedative for transportation (Leitritz and Lewis, 1980). It is extremely soluble in water and the technique simply involves bubbling the gas into the medium. It is inconvenient in that appropriate cylinders and valves are required and furthermore the final concentration of CO_2 in the medium is difficult to control. In a recent study Takeda and Itazawa (1983) concluded that the method was effective but impractical as pO_2 needs to be maintained at elevated levels when pCO_2 is high.

21

Solomon and Hawkins (1981) discuss the effects of dissolved gases during transportation of fish.

The well known anaesthetic "halothane" has been demonstrated to be effective in fish (Langdon, pers. comm.). Dose levels of $0·5$–$2·0$ ml.l^{-1} produce anaesthesia or alternatively the gas can be vaporised and dissolved to effect. Induction is dose related and rapid with excellent maintenance and rapid recovery (2–5 min). Thus although good surgical anaesthesia can be provided, the gas is relatively insoluble in water and consequently the technique is difficult to control and there is also the risk that fish can receive a fatal dose of pure halothane.

CHAPTER 6

Non chemical methods

It is possible to immobilise fish without the use of chemicals and the 2 techniques available, namely hypothermia and electro-anaesthesia may have distinct advantages over chemical methods for certain procedures.

Hypothermia

Temperature influences the activity and oxygen consumption of fish and also the oxygen-carrying capacity of the water. Lowering the water temperature will tranquilise or immobilise fish. Cooling can be achieved by refrigeration or by the addition of ice or by using dry ice in thermal contact with the water but chemically isolated from it (Solomon and Hawkins, 1981).

A given species of fish usually has a fairly wide temperature tolerance. The amount of cooling or heating which can be applied instantaneously to a fish however depends on its previous temperature history and its acclimation temperature. Thus, although hypothermia can immobilise fish and lower the metabolic rate, the degree of cooling which can be applied in a practical situation may be very limited. Various authors have used the technique, principally for transportation (Fish and Hanavan, 1948; Anon, 1982). Some attendant mortalities have been noted and it is not clear whether these can be attributed to excessive cooling or the additive action of chemical anaesthetics with which it is often used.

In practise it has been found that an instantaneous temperature decrease of only 6°C can be applied to tilapia fry acclimated to 25°C, greater rates of decrease producing measurable mortalities. When used in conjunction with chemical anaesthesia (benzocaine) the normally effective dose had to be reduced by about 30% (Okoye, 1982).

Electroanaesthesia (Electroimmobilisation)

A promising alternative to chemical anaesthesia is the use of electricity. Alternating, direct and pulsating currents are all capable of producing immobilisation in fish (Scheminsky, 1934) but their modes of action differ. These current modes have all been used in electrofishing for many years (Vibert, 1967) and all 3 types are suitable for use in freshwater whereas only the latter is fully effective in seawater.

Immobilisation using D.C. is termed galvonarcosis (Halsband, 1967). Kynard and Lonsdale (1975) demonstrated rapid paralysis of yearling rainbow trout subjected to field strengths of 0.6 v.cm^{-1} D.C. The fish move initially towards the anode, lose equilibrium and become immobile in rapid succession (Halsband, 1967). By contrast, tilapia require a D.C. field strength of approximately 3 v.cm^{-1} to produce a similar effect (Ross, unpublished data). Having established immobility it is often subsequently possible to reduce the field strength and in this condition simple procedures can be carried out so long as the fish remains with its head towards the anode and within the applied electrical field. On turning off the current, or if the fish escapes from the electrical field it will recover almost immediately.

Alternating currents, generally derived from the domestic electricity supply, are also effective in inducing anaesthesia, but in this case the effects are not abolished by switching off the supply. Ludwig (1930) and Scheminsky (1934) studied the effects of alternating currents on fish. Ludwig (1930) described 3 successive responses in fish behaviour to increasing electric current. Following initial mild stimulatory effects, electrotaxis occurred and at higher voltages electronarcosis. The reactions of fish to an electric field can differ markedly and depend upon the intensity of the electrical field, the duration of the electrical stimulation and the morphology of the fishes body (Ellis, 1975). The effects of manipulating field strengths and exposure time are exemplified by data on tilapia given in Figure 9. It has been demonstrated that larger fish intercept a greater potential difference than small fish (Holtzer, 1932; Halsband, 1967; Vibert, 1967) and consequently larger fish are effected more rapidly by relatively low potentials than small fish. It has consistently been shown that the single most important factor in this is the head to tail voltage. It should be clear from this that a longer fish will intercept a greater voltage than a smaller one. Consequently, one way in which the anaesthetic effect will be altered is when the fish are not orientated parallel to the direction of electron flow.

The great advantage of electroanaesthesia is reduced netting stress both of the fish and of the operator as rapid immobilisation can be achieved even in relatively large holding facilities. It also has great advantages for biochemical or nutritional studies where the fish may need to be immobilised or even killed instantly. Further it is likely that this technique, when fully refined, will be the method of choice for airbreathing species. It should be noted however, that the physiological effects of electroanaesthesia produce haematological changes broadly similar to those from chemical anaesthesia (Madden and

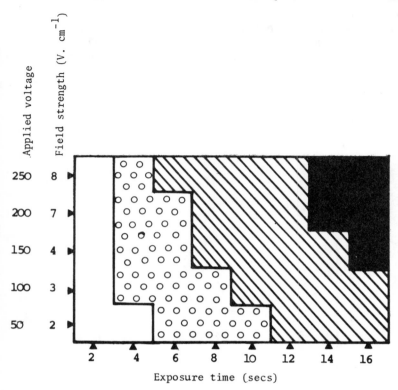

FIG. 9. Effects of electrical field strength and duration of exposure on tilapia. Note that the effects are graded from simple taxis to deep anaesthesia.

Houston, 1976; Schreck *et al.*, 1976). Indeed blood electrolytes and body water distribution may undergo large changes (Schreck *et al.*, 1976) and these may last for a day or more. The technique of immobilising fish using alternating currents is summarised in Appendix 2.

CHAPTER 7

Discussion

In any given situtaion it is always worth reconsidering whether anaesthesia or sedation are strictly necessary. In Chapter 1 a number of instances have been given where anaesthesia may not be essential or whether there are indeed contraindications to its use. Simple fish holders can be constructed which will constrain small specimens quietly, usually for some tens of seconds, allowing rapid tagging or marking. Many broodstock fish can be stripped without recourse to anaesthetics and without damage so long as the handler is gentle but firm. As a general rule it is advisable to avoid the use of chemicals with organisms destined for human consumption for obvious reasons. Thus, although the US Food and Drugs Administration allows the use of MS222 and Quinaldine with cultured fish, they require that no drugs should be used for 21 days prior to sacrifice.

Having decided that some degree of immobilisation is desirable, the selection of a suitable anaesthetic technique will be influenced by the situation in which it will be used and thus no simple guidelines can be given. As this review attempts to show, there are advantages and disadvantages inherent in all of the methods described and these should be weighed against the requirements of the work in hand. In addition to availability of equipment, the availability and cost of drugs may limit the choices. It would be prudent in most cases to have more than 1 drug available, for example using benzocaine as a routine but holding small stocks of MS222 for use when no appropriate organic solvent is available. Field workers may note that judicious use of vodka or gin with benzocaine can overcome solvent problems in emergencies.

Many workers rely on only 1 drug, presumably adhering to the old axiom "better the devil you know than the one you don't". This will serve well in most instances but, again, the pro's and con's of all the available methods should be weighed against the objectives of the work. A single approach will not serve for all ends and it is hoped that this book, at the least, may engender flexibility.

There are considerable practical advantages to be gained by using electrical anaesthetic techniques. Following modest initial outlay, running costs would be relatively low. It should be borne in mind that anaesthetic drugs are frequently expensive, or difficult to obtain in certain parts of the world, whereas electricity will be available or can be made available by the use of inexpensive portable generators. A problem with electrical anaesthesia is that of operator safety and while the use of isolating transformers and interlocking switches can reduce the dangers, it is virtually impossible to guarantee that electric shocks cannot be sustained. It is therefore most important to adhere to a well considered code of practise and although the technique is described for practical implementation in Appendix 2 it should be noted that the authors accept no responsibility for accidents in the use of this equipment, howsoever caused.

It is possible that further research will bring electroanaesthesia into wider use in aquaculture but at present drugs, notably benzocaine, MS222 and quinaldine are used routinely world-wide for most purposes. For more complex procedures and surgical work chemicals are, and will probably remain, the first choice as much more is known of the physiological effects. Table 6 is an attempt to draw together some of the avaliable data on the 3 major drugs in current use in order to provide guidelines for inexperienced operators. It will immediately be realised that a simple table such as this could be greatly expanded, thereby becoming infinitely more useful. The authors would be interested to receive communications regarding problems and experiences.

TABLE 6   Summary of dose rates for a number of fish species using MS222, benzocaine and quinaldine

Drug	Species	Dose	Author
MS222	*Salmo gairdneri*	100 mg/l	Soivio *et al.* (1977)
		80 mg/l	Wedemeyer (1969)
	Salvelinus fontinalis	100 mg/l	Houston *et al.* (1971)
	Oncorhynchus sp	50 mg/l	Strange and Schreck (1978)
	Salmo salar	100 mg/l	Soivio *et al.* (1974)
	Cyprinus carpio	100 mg/l	Houston *et al.* (1973)
	Tinca tinca	25–200 mg/l	Randall (1962)
	Mugil cephalus	20–120 mg/l	Sylvester (1975)
		75–100 mg/l	Dick (1975)
	Tilapia adults	100–200 mg/l	Ross and Geddes (1979)
	Tilapia fry	60–70 mg/l	Ross and Geddes (1979)
Benzocaine	*Salmo gairdneri*	33–50 mg/l	Oswald (1978)
	Salmo trutta	40 mg/l	Oswald (1978)
	Salmo salar	40 mg/l	Ross (unpublished)
	Esox luscius	200 mg/l	Webster (1983)
	Gadus morhua	40 mg/l	Ross (unpublished)
	Pollachius virens	40 mg/l	Ross (unpublished)
	Tilapia species	100 mg/l	Ross and Geddes (1979)
	Clarias batrachus	100 mg/l (+)	Ross and Geddes (1979)
Quinaldine	*Salmo gairdneri*	15 ppm	Julin (1969)
	Various species	10–30 ppm	Tytler and Hawkins (1981)
	Tropical marines	200 ppm	Blasiola (1976)
	Warmwater species	15–70 ppm	Julin (1969)
	Blennius pholis	2·5–20 ppm	Dixon and Milton (1978)
	Lya dussumieri	100 ppm	Sylvester (1975)

REFERENCES

Alexander, R. McN. (1967). *Functional Design in Fishes*. Hutchinson and Co. Ltd., London.

Allison, L. N. (1961). The effect of tricaine methanesulphonate (MS222) on the motility of Brook Trout sperm. *Prog. Fish. Cult.*, **23**, 46–48.

Anon. (1982). Eel exports. *Fish Farmer*, **5(4)**, 29.

Bell, G. R. (1964). A guide to the properties, characteristics, and uses of some general anaesthetics for fish. *Fish. Res. Bd. Can. Bull.*, **148**.

Blasiola, G. C. (1976). Quinaldine sulphate, a new anaesthetic formulation for tropical marine fish. *J. Fish Biol.*, **10(1)**, 113–120.

Casillas, E. and Smith, L. S. (1977). The effect of stress on blood coagulation and haematology in rainbow trout. *J. Fish Biol.*, **10**, 481–491.

Cherkin, A. and Catchpool, J. F. (1964). Temperature dependence of anaesthesia in goldfish. *Science*, **144**, 1460–1461.

Clarke, R. S. J. and Dundee, J. W. (1966). Survey of experimental and clinical pharmacology of propanidid. *Anaesth. Analg. curr. Res.*, **45**, 250–262.

Dick, G. L. (1975). Some observations on the use of MS222 Sandoz with grey mullet (*Mugil chelocuvier*). *J. Fish. Biol.*, **7**, 263–268.

Dixon, R. N. and Milton, P. (1978). Effects of the anaesthetic quinaldine on oxygen consumption in the intertidal teleost *Blennius pholis* (L). *J. Fish. Biol.*, **12**, 359–369.

Ellis, J. E. (1975). Electrotaxic and narcotic responses of channel catfish to various electrical pulse rates and voltage amplitudes. *Prog. Fish. Cult.*, **37(3)**, 155–157.

Fagerlund, U. H. M. and Donaldson, E. M. (1970). Dynamics of cortisone secretion in sockeye salmon (*Oncorhynchus nerka*) during sexual maturation and after gonadectomy. *J. Fish Res. Bd. Can.*, **27**, 2323–2331.

Fish, F. F. and Hanavan, M. G. (1948). A report on the Grand Coulee fish maintenance project (1939–1947). *U.S. Fish Wildlife Serv., Spec. Sci. Rept.*, **55**, 63 pp.

Fryer, J. N. (1975). Stress and adrenocorticosteroid dynamics in the goldfish *Carassius auratus*. *Can. J. Zool.*, **53**, 1012–1020.

Halsband, E. (1967). Basic principles of electric fishing. In *Fishing with Electricity—Its Applications to Biology and Management* (edited by R. Vibert), 276 pp. Fishing News (Books) Ltd., London.

Holzer, W. (1932). Uber die Stromdichte in Forelleri bei galvanischer Durchrommung in Flussigkecht. *Pflugers Arch.*, **232(6)**, 835–841.

Houston, A. H., Madden, J. A., Woods, R. J. and Miles, H. M. (1971). Some physiological effects of handling and tricaine methanesulphonate anaesthetisation upon the Brook Trout, *Salvelinus fontinalis*. *J. Fish Res. Bd. Can.*, **28(5)**, 625–633.

Houston, A. H. and Woods, R. J. (1972). Blood concentrations of tricaine methanesulphonate in Brook Trout, *Salvelinus fontinalis*, during anaesthetisation, branchial irrigation and recovery. *J. Fish Res. Bd. Can.*, **29(9)**, 1344–1346.

Houston, A. H., Czerwinski, C. L. and Woods, R. J. (1973). Cardiovascular and

30

respiratory activity during recovery from anaesthesia and surgery in brook trout (*Salvelinus fontinalis*) and carp (*Cyprinus carpio*). *J. Fish Res. Bd. Can.*, **30**, 1705–1712.

Huish, M. T. (1972). Some responses of the Brown Bullhead (*Ictalurus nebulosus*) to MS222. *Prog. Fish Cult.*, **34(1)**, 27–32.

Julin. (1975).

Kynard, B. and Lonsdale, E. (1975). Experimental study of galvonarcosis for rainbow trout (*Salmo gairdneri*) immobilisation. *J. Fish Res. Bd. Can.*, **32**, 300–302.

Laird, L. M. and Oswald, R. L. (1975). A note on the use of benzocaine (ethyl-p-aminobenzoate) as a fish anaesthetic. *J. Inst. Fish Mgt.*, **6**, 92–94.

Leitritz, E. and Lewis, R. C. (1980). Trout and salmon culture (hatchery methods). *Cal. Fish Bull.*, **164**, Univ. of Calif., 197 pp.

Ludwig, N. (1930). Uber electrotaxis und elektronarkose von Fischen. *Pflugers Arch.*, **244(2)**, 268–277.

Madden, J. and Houston, A. (1976). Use of electroanaesthesia with freshwater teleosts: some physiological consequences in the rainbow trout, *Salmo gairdneri*, Richardson. *J. Fish Biol.*, **9(6)**, 457–462.

McFarland, W. N. (1959). A study of the effects of anaesthetics on the behaviour and physiology of fishes. *Pub. Inst. Marine Sci.*, **6**, 22–55.

McFarland, W. N. and Klontz, G. W. (1969). Anaesthesia in fishes. *Fed. Proc.*, **28(4)**, 1535–1540.

Nakatani, R. E. (1962). A method for force-feeding radio-isotope to yearling trout. *Proc. Fish Cult.*, **24**, 156–160.

Okoye, R. N. (1982). *Techniques for Transportation of Juvenile Tilapia*, 39 pp. M.Sc. Thesis, Univ. Stirling.

Oswald, R. L. (1978). Injection anaesthesia for experimental studies in fish. *Comp. Biochem. Pyhsiol.*, **60C**, 19–26.

Pauling, L. (1961). A molecular theory of general anaesthesia. *Science*, **134**, 15–21.

Randall, D. J. (1962). Effect of anaesthetic on the heart and respiration of a teleost fish. *Nature. Lond.*, **195**, 506.

Randall, D. J. (1970). The circulatory system. In *Fish Physiology Vol. IV. The Nervous System, Circulation and Respiration* (edited by W. S. Hoare and D. J. Randall), Academic Press.

Randall, D. J. and Smith, L. S. (1967). The effect of environmental factors on circulation and respiration in teleost fish. *Hydrobiologia*, **29**, 113–124.

Ross, L. G. and Wiewiorka, J. (1977). An audible low-cost heart rate monitor for use in fish surgery. *Laboratory Practise*, **26**, 188.

Ross, L. G. and Geddes, J. A. (1979). Sedation of warm water fish species in aquaculture research. *Aquaculture*, **16**, 183–186.

Ross, B. and Ross, L. G. (1983). The oxygen requirements of *Oreochromis niloticus* under adverse conditions. *Proc. 1st Int. Symp. on Tilapia in Aquaculture*. Nazareth, Israel, (in press).

Scheminsky, F. (1934). Uber die Naturder Wechselstromnarkose bei Fischen. *Arb. Ungar. Biol. Forschungsinst.*, **6**, 209–211.

Schoettger, R. A. and Steucke, E. W. (1970). Quinaldine and MS222 as spawning aids for Northern Pike, Muskellunge and Walleyes. *Prog. Fish Cult.*, **82(4)**, 199–205.

Schreck, C. B., Whaley, R. H., Bass, M. L., Manglon, O. E. and Solazzi, M. (1970). physiological responses of rainbow trout (*Salmo gairdneri*) to electroshock. *J. Fish Res. Bd. Can.*, **33(1)**, 76–84.

Sehdev, H. S., McBride, J. R. and Fagerlund, U. H. M. (1963). 2-phenoxyethanol as a general anaesthetic for Sockeye Salmon. *J. Fish Res. Bd. Can.*, **20**, 1435–1440.

Serfaty, A., Labat, R. and Quillier, R. (1959). Les reactions cardiaques chez la carpe (*Cyprinus carpio*) au cours d'une anaesthesie prolongee. *Hydrobiologia*, **13**, 134–151.

Singley, J. A. and Chavin, W. (1975). The adrenocortical—hypophysial response to saline stress in the goldfish, *Carassius auratus* L. *Comp. Biochem. Physiol.*, **51A**, 749–756.

Smith, L. S. (1982). *Introduction to Fish Physiology*, 352 pp. T. F. H. Publications.

Soivio, A., Malkonen, M. and Tuurala, O. (1974). Effects of asphyxia and MS222 anaesthesia on the circulation of the kidney in *S. gairdneri. Richardson. Ann. Zool. Fenn.*, **11**, 271–275.

Soivio, A., Nyholm, K. and Huhti, M. (1977). Effects of anaesthesia with MS222, neutralised MS222 and benzocaine on the blood constituents of Rainbow Trout. *J. Fish. Biol.*, **10**, 91–101.

Solomon, D. J. and Hawkins, A. D. (1981). Fish capture and transport. In *Aquarium Systems* (edited by A. D. Hawkins), Academic Press.

Sprague, J. B. (1971). Measurement of pollutant toxicity to fish. III. Sublethal effects and "safe" concentrations. *Water research*, **5**, 245–266.

Strange, J. R. and Schreck, C. B. (1978). Anaesthetic and handling stress on survival and cortisol concentrations in yearling chinook salmon (*Oncorhynchus tschawytscha*). *J. Fish Res. Bd. Can.*, **35**, 345–349.

Stuart, N. C. (1979). *A Critical Review of the Literature on the Anaesthesia of Fishes*, 111 pp. M.Sc. Thesis, Univ. Stirling.

Sylvester, J. R. (1975). Factors influencing the efficacy of MS222 to striped mullet (*Mugil cephalus*). *Aquaculture*, **6**, 163–169.

Takeda, T. and Itzawa, Y. (1983). Examination of the possibility in applying anaesthesia by carbon dioxide in the transportation of live fish. *Bull. Jap. Soc. Sci. Fish.*, **49(5)**, 725–732.

Tytler, P. and Hawkins, A. D. (1981). Vivisection, anaesthetics and minor surgery. In *Aquarium Systems* (edited by A. D. Hawkins), Academic Press.

Vibert, R. (1967). *Fishing with Electricity*, 276 pp. Fishing News (Books) Ltd., London.

Walker, M. D. (1972). Physiologic and pharmacologic aspects of barbiturates in Elasmobranchs. *Comp. Biochem. Physiol.*, **42A**, 213–221.

Wardle, C. S. (1972). The changes in blood glucose in *Pleuronectes platessa* following capture from the wild: a stress reaction. *J. mar. biol. Ass. U.K.*, **52**, 635–651.

Wardle, C. S. and Kanwisher, J. W. (1974). The significance of heart rate in free-swimming Cod, *Gadus morhua*: some observations with ultrasonic tags. *Mar. Behav. Physiol.*, **2**, 311–324.

Webster, J. (1983). *The Swimbladder as a Hydrostatic Organ in the Northern Pike*, Esox luscius (L). Ph.D. Thesis, Univ. Stirling.

Wedemeyer, G. (1969). Stress-induced ascorbic acid depletion and cortisol production in two salmonid fishes. *Comp. Biochem. Physiol.*, **29**, 1247–1251.

Wedemeyer, G. (1970). The role of stress in the disease resistance of fishes. *Am. Fish. Soc. Symp. on Disease of Fish and Shellfish*, Spec. Publ. No 5.

Wood, E. M. (1956). Urethane as a carcinogen. *Proc. Fish. Cult.*, **18**, 135.

Yaron, Z., Ilan, Z., Bogomolnaya, J. and Vermaak, P. (1983). Steroid hormones in two tilapia species *Oreochromis aureus* and *O. Niloticus. Proc. 1st Int. Symp. on Tilapia in Aquaculture*, Nazareth, Israel, (in press).

APPENDIX 1

Method for inhalation anaesthesia using benzocaine

Procedure to be followed for simple handling where no artificial ventilation is required.

1. Prepare stock solution of benzocaine, usually 100 g benzocaine dissolved in 1 litre of ethanol or acetone. Store in a dark bottle.
2. Prepare anaesthetic bath to appropriate final concentration (see table 6) by slowly adding stock solution to water with thorough stirring to prevent the drug coming out of solution.
3. Prepare a recovery vessel of clean, well-oxygenated water.
4. Ensure that both the stock tank, anaesthetic bath and recovery vessel are all at the same temperature. Adjust if necessary.
5. Ensure that all relevant equipment for the intended technique is prepared and ready to hand before proceeding further.
6. Quickly net out a small batch of fish from stock and transfer immediately to the anaesthetic bath. The number of fish per batch will depend on the time taken to handle each fish. On no account should the fish remain in the bath for extended periods. As a rough guide fish should not remain in the anaesthetic bath for longer than 10 min.
7. For simple procedures it is usually possible to achieve adequate handling before the fish have lost equilibrium. Operations should commence as soon as a fish can be picked up without struggling.
8. After handling the fish should be placed immediately in the recovery tank. Substantial recovery will normally occur within 1 min, although some species may require slightly longer. On no account should the recovery tank be allowed to become overstocked.

APPENDIX 2

Method for electroanaesthesia using alternating current

1. The most convenient A.C. source is the domestic mains or a portable generator providing an equivalent of the domestic mains. The available voltage will thus be in the region of 240–250 v A.C.
2. The critical factor for successful electroanaesthesia is to achieve a uniform field density and some minimum size-dependent head to tail voltage. Uniform field density will best be achieved in a rectangular tank with rectangular stainless steel electrodes placed at each end. Users need to experiment with other shapes of

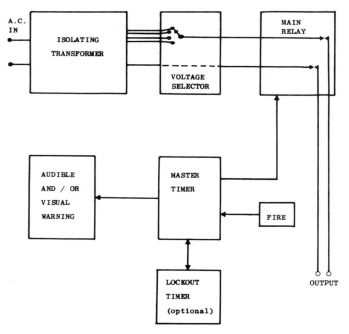

Fig. 10.   Schematic diagram of minimum electrical system required for electro-anaesthesia.

34

tank, and field density can be made more uniform by using multiple electrodes. The maximum length of the tank must not be such as to reduce the head to tail voltage of the fish size being used to less than that required for immobilisation.

3. Arrange for tank with the electrodes firmly clamped at each end and in such a way that the fish cannot swim behind the electrodes.

4. Safety is of paramount importance and the voltage should be applied to the electrodes via an isolating transformer of modest current capacity thus protecting the operator to some extent. An appropriate isolating transformer will normally have a series of secondary tappings which can be switched thus giving some control over the total applied voltage.

5. It may be possible to time the application of the voltage using a stopwatch, but this is more reliably achieved using a simple electronic timer controlling the switch.

6. In addition to these minimum requirements, as much protection as possible should be afforded to those in the vicinity of the operation. This can be achieved by the use of serial lock-out switches on the control box and by the use of audible warning signals and flashing lights.

7. It should be noted that there can be no total protection system for operators and consequently a rigid code of practice should be enforced.

Lake Turkana

A Report of the Findings of the Lake Turkana Project
1972–1975

Edited by A. J. Hopson

Published by

Institute of Aquaculture, University of Stirling

---

* Price Hardback Edition: £160   * Price Paperback Edition: £85
(with gold blocking)   (with lifeguard cover)

Lake Turkana, in North West Kenya, is the last of the great lakes of the world to be scientifically studied. This series of six large format volumes sets out the detailed findings of the major survey of the lake, funded by the British Government on behalf of the Government of Kenya. It comprises thirteen chapters and two appendices describing the Biology, Limnology, Geography, Bathymetry, Climatology and Chemistry of Lake Turkana, its Fishes and Fisheries and its potential in terms of Fishery Management.

The Book is profusely illustrated with colour and black and white photographs and line drawings, and a special feature is the set of sixty plates, in taxonomic detail, of the major fish species found in the lake.

6 volumes   ISBN 0-901636-41-X   1,900 pages

* Prices include Postage (air parcel) and Packing.

A Guide to Tilapia Feeds and Feeding

by

Kim Jauncey and Barbara Ross

with a foreword by

Mr. J. Stoneman

(Fisheries Adviser: Overseas Development Administration)

Published by

Institute of Aquaculture, University of Stirling

---

* 111 pp.   1 volume   £9.50

The intensive culture of tilapias is a relatively new development and it is important that any approaches to understanding their food requirements are related to the very distinct feeding behaviour of these specialised fishes. The purpose of this handbook (now in its second printing) is to provide all of the currently available practical information to allow the formulation and manufacture of complete or supplementary feeds for cultured tilapias.

All of the known nutritional requirements of the genera are outlined and where such information is fragmentary, or more often, completely lacking, guidelines are given based on the requirements of similar fish species.

The book comprises 111 pages and includes 1 plate, 8 figures and 17 tables.

* Prices include Postage (air parcel) and Packing.

Tilapia: A guide to their biology and culture in Africa

by J. D. Balarin and J. P. Hatton
(1979 reprinted 1981)

Published by Institute of Aquaculture, University of Stirling

174 pages   Price £10 (surface mail).   ISBN 0-901636-23-1

This book has become the standard text for all seeking background to the culture of these, the most important of tropical farmed species. Chapters detail the biology, nutrition, water requirements and culture techniques reported from both Africa and Asia, and discuss the opportunities for further expansion of Tilapia culture.

A Bibliography of *Anguilla* spp
(Pisces : Teleostei)

by E. W. Liewes
(with a preface by Dr. C. L. Deelder)

In two volumes, 1980.   471 pages

Price £20 (surface mail).   ISBN   0-901636-30-4/31-2

The eels are among the most written about and yet least understood of all farmed and wild fishes. In this set of two volumes, Dr. Liewes has garnered all of the references that are available, in a variety of languages, up to 1980, detailing fascinating biology of this unusual group.

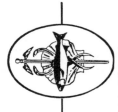